W9-AJQ-132

A *FOR BETTER OR FOR WORSE*® COLLECTION

STARTING FROM SCRATCH

BY LYNN JOHNSTON

Andrews and McMeel
A Universal Press Syndicate Company
Kansas City

105789   Eau Claire District Library

FOR BETTER OR FOR WORSE® is distributed internationally by Universal Press Syndicate.

STARTING FROM SCRATCH copyright © 1995 by Lynn Johnston Productions, Inc. All rights reserved. Printed in the United States of America. No part of this book may be used or reproduced in any manner whatsoever without written permission except in the case of reprints in the context of reviews. For information write Andrews and McMeel, a Universal Press Syndicate Company, 4900 Main Street, Kansas City, Missouri 64112.

ISBN: 0-8362-0424-7

Library of Congress Catalog Card Number: 95-77570

——— ATTENTION: SCHOOLS AND BUSINESSES ———

Andrews and McMeel books are available at quantity discounts with bulk purchase for educational, business, or sales promotional use. For information, please write to: Special Sales Department, Andrews and McMeel, 4900 Main Street, Kansas City, Missouri 64112.

741.5
Joh
pb

STARTING
FROM SCRATCH

WITHDRAWN

 Eau Claire District Library

14

15

MICHAEL... GRADUATING ALREADY! – YOU KNOW, MOM? IT HARDLY SEEMS POSSIBLE!

HE'S KNOWN MOST OF THOSE KIDS SINCE HE WAS 6. IN A FEW WEEKS, THEY'LL ALL BE GONE IN DIFFERENT DIRECTIONS. SOME OF THEM, HE WILL NEVER SEE AGAIN.

IT'S A TIME FOR GOODBYES, A TIME FOR REFLECTION. – RIGHT NOW, HE'LL BE HAVING SOME PRETTY EMOTIONAL THOUGHTS ABOUT HIS SCHOOL.

MAN, I CAN'T WAIT TO **BLOW** THIS JOINT!!!

HEY, WANNA RIDE?

SURE, LAWRENCE. THANKS!

I GOT ACCEPTED AT THE AGRICULTURAL COLLEGE IN OTTAWA, MIKE!

LOOKS LIKE I'LL BE GOING TO LONDON.

I REALLY WANNA MOVE, YOU KNOW? I JUST WANT TO BE ON MY OWN FOR A CHANGE.

ME TOO. – I DON'T MIND LEAVING THIS PLACE.

... AS LONG AS EVERYTHING'S STILL HERE WHEN I GET BACK.

SLAM! THANKS! – SEE YOU LATER!

GOOD OLD FARLEY...

– HE DOESN'T JUST WAG HIS TAIL WHEN YOU COME HOME .... HE WAGS EVERYTHING!

MICHAEL, YOU ARE NOT WEARING JEANS TO YOUR GRADUATION!!

BUT, MOM - OUR GOWNS COVER WHAT WE'RE WEARING!

HEY, IT'S NO BIG DEAL!! YOU COULD BE STARK NAKED UNDER THAT THING, AN' NOBODY'D KNOW!

I DON'T CARE!

I WANT YOU TO WEAR A SHIRT, A DECENT PAIR OF PANTS AND GOOD SHOES. - THIS IS A SOLEMN AND IMPORTANT OCCASION!!

...AT WHICH 250 PEOPLE WILL BE WEARING FUNNY HATS.

Lynn

OK, GRADUATES, YOU WILL ASSEMBLE HERE FIRST, AND, WHEN THE AUDIENCE IS SEATED, THE MUSIC WILL START AND YOU WILL ENTER IN SINGLE FILE, FILLING THE FIRST 8 ROWS OF THE AUDITORIUM.

AFTER THE OPENING SPEECHES, WE WILL CALL YOU ONTO THE STAGE IN ALPHABETICAL ORDER. YOU WILL ENTER FROM THE RIGHT, SHAKE HANDS WITH THE PRINCIPAL, ACCEPT YOUR DIPLOMA, AND EXIT TO THE LEFT.

UH, LIKE, THAT MEANS WE, LIKE, GO UP AN' GET IT, AN' SIT DOWN AGAIN?

CORRECT.

LOOK OUT, WORLD... THEY'RE ALL YOURS NOW.

Lynn

AS WE LEAVE THESE HALLOWED HALLS, WE NOT ONLY TAKE WITH US OUR EDUCATION... BUT WE TAKE WITH US OUR FRIENDSHIPS AND OUR MEMORIES. THESE THINGS WE WILL CHERISH FOREVER, IN OUR MINDS AND IN OUR HEARTS..

AND TODAY... AS WE STAND ON THE THRESHOLD OF OUR FUTURE, WE MUST LOOK INTO OUR HEARTS_ AND WE MUST ASK OURSELVES....

DOESN'T ONE GUY HERE HAVE A SPITBALL?

Lynn

21

I'LL CALL AND CANCEL THE NEW FURNITURE, JOHN.

THERE'S NO NEED TO DO THAT. WE'RE O.K.

I CAN'T BELIEVE I LOST MY JOB!—IT WASN'T EXACTLY FULL TIME, AND IT DIDN'T PAY A GREAT DEAL, BUT I ENJOYED IT. I IDENTIFIED WITH IT!

I MEAN,... WITHOUT A JOB— WHO AM I?

MUM!

THAT'S THE WAY IT GOES, EL. THERE ARE HUGE BUDGET RESTRAINTS AT THE HOSPITAL. EVERYONE'S AFRAID THAT THE NEXT CUTBACK WILL INCLUDE THEM.

YOU WOULDN'T BELIEVE THE BICKERING THAT GOES ON.—IT'S THE TENSION. SOMETIMES IT REALLY GETS TO YOU.

EVERY DAY, I COME HOME TIRED AND CRABBY... AND WHAT FOR? —WHY DON'T WE ALL JUST QUIT THIS RAT RACE, MOVE TO SOME DESERT ISLAND, AND BECOME HERMITS? WHY DON'T WE START ENJOYING LIFE?!!

... THERE'S NO MONEY IN IT.

I THINK MICHAEL'S RIGHT, MOM. MAYBE LOSING YOUR JOB AT THE LIBRARY WAS A GOOD THING.

YOU KNOW HOW THEY SAY "WHEN ONE DOOR CLOSES, ANOTHER ONE OPENS"... WELL, MAYBE THAT'S TRUE FOR YOU!

MAYBE THERE'S AN OPEN DOOR THAT WILL GIVE YOU, LIKE, SOMETHING TOTALLY NEW TO FOCUS ON!

40

Panel 1: GROAN! ...I ACHE ALL OVER!
I'M NOT SURPRISED, EL!

Panel 2: YOU EXERCISED PRETTY HARD YESTERDAY.... AND YOU'RE NOT USED TO IT.

Panel 3: YOU SHOULD WORK UP TO THESE THINGS SLOWLY, START WITH SOMETHING THAT'S PLEASANT AND COMFORTING AND EASY TO DO.
LIKE WHAT?

Panel 4: WELL... I COULD USE A BACKRUB!!

Panel 5: CHUCK, KEEP, CHUCK, KEEP, KEEP, CHUCK.....

Panel 6: CHUCK, CHUCK, KEEP, CH....

Panel 8: ...TAKE WITH ME.

Panel 9: PACKING ALREADY? BUT, YOU DON'T LEAVE FOR LONDON FOR A WHILE YET.
I KNOW.

Panel 10: I JUST WANTED TO SORT THROUGH MY STUFF.... DECIDE WHAT I'M TAKING, WHAT I WANT TO THROW OUT.

Panel 11: IT'S GOING TO BE SO DIFFERENT WITHOUT YOU, HONEY, SO QUIET, SO....
HEY, DON'T THINK OF IT AS "LOSING A SON," MOM!

Panel 12: —THINK OF IT AS "GAINING A SPARE ROOM"!

Panel 1: IT'S NOT AS THOUGH I'LL BE LEAVING FOR GOOD! I'LL BE HOME ON HOLIDAYS AN' STUFF!

I KNOW.

Panel 2: ...IT'S JUST THAT I WORRY. WHEN KIDS ARE ON THEIR OWN, THINGS HAPPEN. THEY SOMETIMES GET CARRIED AWAY. THEY PARTY. THEY EXPERIMENT. THEY DO THINGS THEY WOULDN'T ORDINARILY DO!

Panel 3: HEY, MOM—NOT TO WORRY!... YOU KNOW THE OLD SAYING...

Panel 4: "YOU HAVE NOTHING TO FEAR, BUT BEER ITSELF!"

Panel 5: WHATCHA THINKING ABOUT, LIZ?

MY BROTHER. HE'S GONNA BE LEAVING SOON.

Panel 6: THAT MEANS YOU'RE NOT GONNA GET CALLED "LIZARDBREATH" ANYMORE!

YEAH.

Panel 7: AN' NO MORE HASSLES ABOUT THE PHONE! YOU DON'T HAFTA WORRY ABOUT BEIN' TEASED OR BUGGED OR DUMPED ON!

I KNOW.

Panel 8: ....I'M GOING TO MISS HIM.

Panel 9: IT'S COOL, BEING OUTSIDE IN THE WILDERNESS, ISN'T IT, LIZ!

TOTALLY!

Panel 10: LISTEN. IT'S SO QUIET. ALL YOU CAN HEAR IS THE WIND AND THE BIRDS AND THE SOUND OF THE RIVER.

Panel 11: ...IT'S LIKE A WHOLE BEAUTIFUL, PEACEFUL, SPECIAL WORLD!

YEAH!

Panel 12: TOO BAD IT HASTA HAVE PEOPLE IN IT!

44

Panel 1: PATERSON ... PATERSON ... UH, WITH TWO T'S. / RIGHT.

Panel 2: OH-KAY! I'VE GOT YOUR RESIDENCE KEY HERE. CAN I SEE YOUR STUDENT I.D.? / I DON'T HAVE IT YET.

Panel 3: THEN YOU'LL HAVE TO LINE UP OVER THERE FOR PHOTO-GRAPHS, WAIT FOR YOUR CARD, THEN LINE UP AGAIN OVER HERE.

Panel 4: 1 HOUR LATER ... STRANGE. - NOBODY EVER SMILES IN THESE PICTURES!

Panel 5: 17D, 17C ... HERE IT IS!

Panel 6: THIS IS IT. THIS IS WHERE I'M GOING TO LIVE FOR THE NEXT 2 YEARS.

Panel 7: I'VE GOT TO DO SOMETHING TO MAKE IT LOOK MORE LIKE "HOME".

Panel 8: DUMP!

Panel 9: THAT'S PATERSON. WITH TWO T'S. / YES. REGISTRATION FOR FIRST YEAR JOURNALISM IS NOW IN ROOM 103.

Panel 10: HERE'S YOUR BOOK LIST. TAKE YOUR STUDENT CARD AND RECEIPTS TO THE BOOKSTORE AND GO TO LINE TWO.

Panel 11: LINEUPS! EVERYWHERE YOU GO, THERE'S A LINEUP! ... I THINK I'LL TAKE A BREAK AND GRAB A COFFEE.

49

50

FOUR PLACES TO SET AT THE TABLE INSTEAD OF FIVE.

THREE BEDROOMS TO TIDY INSTEAD OF FOUR... THERE'S LESS LAUNDRY TO DO, TOO.

WITH MICHAEL GONE, LIFE'S LESS COMPLICATED. THE CHORES ARE A LITTLE EASIER. THERE'S LESS TO WORRY ABOUT. THERE'S LESS TO DO!

STRANGE... I NEVER THOUGHT A LIGHTER LOAD WOULD FEEL SO HEAVY!

Lynn

YOU MISS MICHAEL, DON'T YOU, MOM.

I KEEP WALKING INTO HIS ROOM, EXPECTING TO SEE HIS STUFF ALL OVER THE FLOOR, EXPECTING TO FIND HIS BED UNMADE AND HIS DRAWERS A SHAMBLES.

BUT EVERYTHING'S IN ORDER. I'M NOT USED TO SEEING IT LIKE THIS!

YEAH.

IF IT MAKES YOU FEEL ANY BETTER, I CAN LEAVE MY ROOM TRASHED !!

Lynn

FLOWERS? FOR ME ?!!

THANK YOU, HONEY! ...I THOUGHT YOU NEEDED A LITTLE CHEERING UP!

WATCH DIS, MOM! WATCH DIS !!

CLOP!

DADDY'S A GOOD CATCH, ISN'T HE!

YES, APRIL, HE'S A VERY GOOD CATCH !!

Lynn

59

62

FOUR BRAND-NEW PUPPIES! CONGRATULATIONS, SERA— YOU'RE A **MOM!**

SHE SEEMS TO KNOW WHAT SHE'S DOING, EL. IT'S AMAZING HOW QUICKLY SHE CAUGHT ON!

WHAT'S **DAT**?!!

IT'S THE UMBILICAL CORD, APRIL. THAT'S THE PUPPY'S BELLY-BUTTON!

IT IS?!

DAD! DAD! GUESS WHAT! **DOGS GOTS BELLY BUTTONS!!**

THESE ARE FARLEY'S PUPPIES, TOO...

SHOULDN'T WE LET HIM SEE THEM?

I'M NOT SURE, LIZ. IT MIGHT NOT BE A GOOD IDEA.

WHEN PUPS ARE BORN, THE MALE REALLY DOESN'T HAVE MUCH TO DO WITH THEM.

THE CARE AND FEEDING IS USUALLY LEFT ENTIRELY UP TO THE MOTHER.

WHAT ARE YOU LOOKING AT ME LIKE THAT FOR?

YOU KNOW, EL, I'VE WORKED IN THE HOSPITAL LAB FOR A LONG TIME... AND I MUST HAVE SEEN THOUSANDS OF NEWBORN BABIES.

BUT EVERY TIME A LITTLE LIFE COMES INTO THE WORLD, I CAN'T HELP THINKING WHAT A MIRACLE IT IS!!

...TWO MICROSCOPIC CELLS COMBINE TO FORM A WHOLE NEW, LIVING ENTITY! DOESN'T THAT SEEM IMPOSSIBLE? DOESN'T THAT SEEM HARD TO BELIEVE?

YES...

— EXCEPT ON THE DAY OF DELIVERY.

80

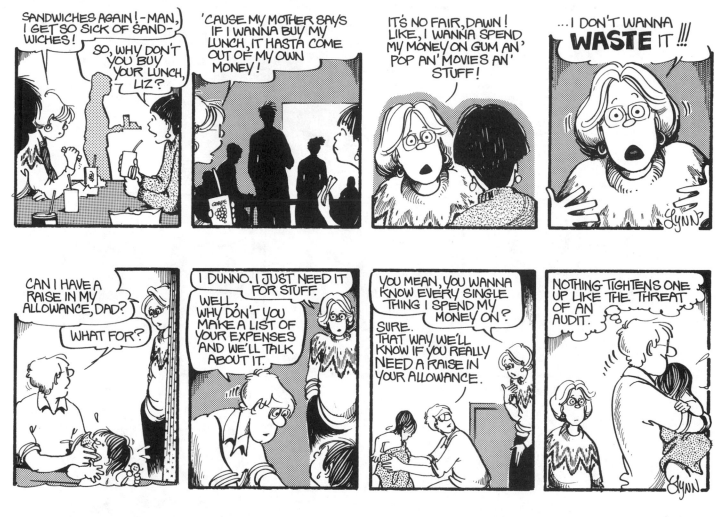

84

PUFF, PUFF, WHEEZE PUFF!

(PUFF, PUFF) OK, I KNOW, I'M SORRY I'M LATE COMIN' HOME AFTER SCHOOL, I (GASP) WENT TO THE MALL WITH SOME FRIENDS, 'CAUSE, WELL, YOU'RE WORKING AGAIN, AN' I DIDN'T WANNA COME HOME 'CAUSE THE HOUSE WAS EMPTY, SO I JUST WENT WITH THEM!

...MOM?

— AN' I NEVER PHONED. SO, I'M IN BIG TROUBLE, RIGHT? MOM?

... WHAT ARE YOU GOING TO DO TO ME?

WHEN I TOOK THE JOB AT THE BOOKSTORE, I DIDN'T THINK ELIZABETH WOULD MIND BEING HOME ALONE AFTER SCHOOL, CONNIE.

I WAS SO EXCITED ABOUT GOING BACK TO WORK AGAIN, I JUST ASSUMED SHE WOULD BE OK.

SHE'S GOING TO GO OVER TO HER FRIEND DAWN'S FROM NOW ON, SO THAT'S SETTLED .... BUT I FEEL SO **GUILTY**!!

WE ALL DO, EL!

WHEN A MOTHER EARNS AN INCOME — THAT'S THE PRICE SHE ALWAYS PAYS.

MOM! COME DOWNSTAIRS AN' SEE THE PUPPIES! SEE HOW BIG THEY ARE!

I LIKE DIS ONE. HE'S MY FAVORITE. CONNIE LETS ME PLAY WIF HIM!

PUT HIM DOWN, NOW HONEY.

HE'S A STRONG LITTLE GUY, EL. APRIL ISN'T GOING TO HURT HIM.

I KNOW...

I JUST DON'T WANT THOSE TWO TO GET ATTACHED.

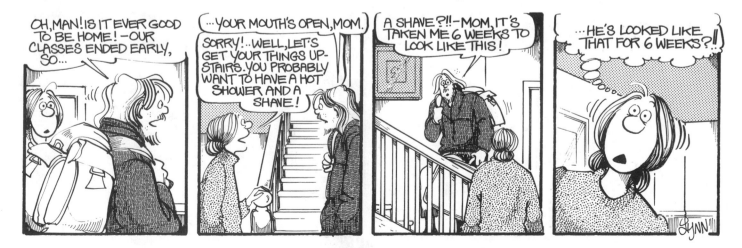

95

I WISH YOU DIDN'T HAVE TO GO SO SOON.

I KNOW. I REALLY HATE THIS.

WHEN YOU'RE IN LONDON, I THINK ABOUT YOU SO MUCH, I MISS YOU SO MUCH, SOMETIMES I THINK I'LL GO CRAZY!

ME TOO!

BUT I'M HERE FOR A FEW MORE HOURS... SO LET'S MAKE EVERY SECOND COUNT.

WHONK! HONK! BEEEP!

ARE MY BAGS DOWNSTAIRS, MOM?

THEY'RE ALL PACKED AND READY TO GO BY THE FRONT DOOR.

I WASHED AND FOLDED YOUR LAUNDRY, I MENDED YOUR BACKPACK, I PUT NOTEPAPER AND STAMPED, SELF-ADDRESSED ENVELOPES IN THE SIDE POUCH — I FIXED THE ZIPPER ON YOUR JACKET, AND PUT A CHEQUE IN THE POCKET.

DID YOU GET HIS BUS TICKET?

OF COURSE NOT!!

— HOW IS HE GOING TO SURVIVE IN THIS WORLD IF WE DO EVERYTHING FOR HIM!!?

97

Panel 1:
WHAT'S THIS WE'RE HAVING?
IT'S CALLED "BEAN MEDLEY CASSEROLE" AND IT'S FROM THE "NEW AGE HEALTH AND FITNESS BIBLE."

Panel 2:
ACCORDING TO THIS BOOK, A VEGETARIAN DIET WOULD MAKE US FEEL HEALTHIER. I THOUGHT WE SHOULD TRY IT!

Panel 3:
COME ON, JUST FOR A WHILE! — NOT GETTING OUR PROTEIN FROM MEAT WILL BE A WHOLE NEW EXPERIENCE!
NO MEAT?

Panel 4:
...YOU MEAN, WE'RE GIVING IT UP FOR LENTIL?

Panel 5:
ELLY, YOU'RE NOT REALLY GOING VEGETARIAN!
I WANNA TRY IT, CONNIE — SEE HOW IT GOES!

Panel 6:
DO YOU THINK JOHN AND THE KIDS WILL BE OK WITH THIS? I MEAN, HOW MANY WAYS CAN YOU COOK BEANS?

Panel 7:
THEY'RE LOOKING FORWARD TO IT, CONNIE. FOR THEM IT POSES A NEW AND EXCITING CHALLENGE.

Panel 8:
(PORK PUFFS)

Panel 9:

WOOF! WOOF! WOOF!
YIP!

Panel 10:
LOOKIT EDGAR, DAD! — HE'S STANDING RIGHT UNDER FARLEY!

Panel 11:

EDGAR'S A SMART DOG!
WHY DO YOU SAY THAT?
WOOF!

Panel 12:

IN WEATHER LIKE THIS, IT'S NICE TO HAVE A WOOF OVER YOUR HEAD!

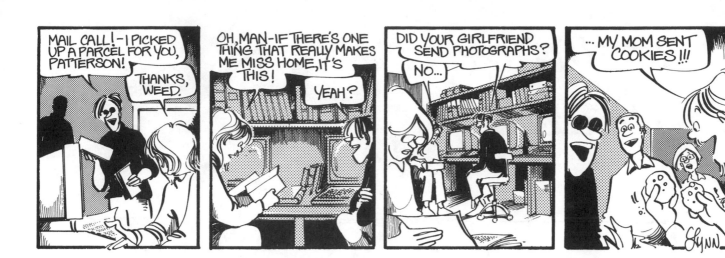

106

Panel 1: G'MORNING, DOC! QUÉ PASA? / OH... NOTHING. ELLY AND I HAD A SLIGHT DISAGREEMENT LAST NIGHT.

Panel 2: A COUPLE OF WEEKS AGO, I AGREED TO TRY A VEGETARIAN DIET. YOU KNOW, TO SEE IF WE FELT BETTER OR SOMETHING!

Panel 3: IT WAS ELLY'S IDEA. I DID IT FOR HER!—AND, I REALLY TRIED, JEAN, BUT GIVING UP MEAT ISN'T EASY! / WHAT MADE YOU GO OFF THE WAGON?

Panel 4: TED ASKED ME IF IT WAS HARD TO QUIT COLD TURKEY.... / ...AND I LOST IT.

Panel 5: THERE'S NOT MUCH HAPPENING IN THE STORE RIGHT NOW, ELLY. WOULD YOU AND MOIRA LIKE TO GO FOR LUNCH? / SURE!

Panel 6: SO, HERE I AM, KNOCKING MYSELF OUT, MAKING NICE, INTERESTING VEGETARIAN MEALS—AND HE SNEAKS OUT AND HAS FRIED CHICKEN!!

Panel 7: WELL, YOU CAN'T BLAME HIM, EL. IT'S AWFULLY HARD TO GIVE UP THE STUFF YOU LOVE TO EAT. I MEAN, WHEN I'M ON A DIET, JUST THE SMELL OF SOME THINGS DRIVES ME **CRAZY**!!

Panel 8: TEX MEX

Panel 9: A BEEF CHIMICHANGA, WITH ALL THE TRIMMINGS, EL? / IF JOHN CAN CHEAT ON OUR DIET, THEN SO CAN I.

Panel 10: LOOK, IT'S OK TO EAT THIS STUFF ONCE IN AWHILE.... YOU DON'T HAVE TO BE A STRICT VEGETARIAN TO BE HEALTHY! / I KNOW, BUT I WANTED TO GIVE IT A TRY.

Panel 11: WOULDN'T IT BE WONDERFUL IF WE COULD JUST EAT EVERYTHING WE LIKE, AND NOT FEEL GUILTY ABOUT IT, MOIRA? / YEAH. HAVING ALL THIS FOOD TO CHOOSE FROM IS A REAL PROBLEM!

Panel 12: BUT YOU KNOW, EL—WHEN YOU THINK ABOUT IT..... IT'S A PROBLEM THAT SOME OF US ARE PRETTY LUCKY TO HAVE!!

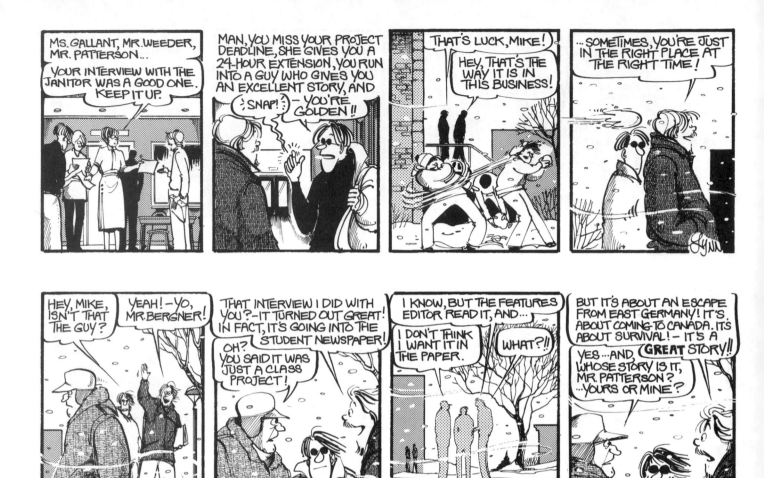

Panel 1:
MS. GALLANT, MR. WEEDER, MR. PATTERSON...

YOUR INTERVIEW WITH THE JANITOR WAS A GOOD ONE. KEEP IT UP.

Panel 2:
MAN, YOU MISS YOUR PROJECT DEADLINE, SHE GIVES YOU A 24-HOUR EXTENSION, YOU RUN INTO A GUY WHO GIVES YOU AN EXCELLENT STORY, AND —SNAP!— YOU'RE GOLDEN!!

Panel 3:
THAT'S LUCK, MIKE!

HEY, THAT'S THE WAY IT IS IN THIS BUSINESS!

Panel 4:
...SOMETIMES, YOU'RE JUST IN THE RIGHT PLACE AT THE RIGHT TIME!

Panel 5:
HEY, MIKE, ISN'T THAT THE GUY?

YEAH! —YO, MR. BERGNER!

Panel 6:
THAT INTERVIEW I DID WITH YOU? —IT TURNED OUT GREAT! IN FACT, IT'S GOING INTO THE STUDENT NEWSPAPER!

OH? YOU SAID IT WAS JUST A CLASS PROJECT!

Panel 7:
I KNOW, BUT THE FEATURES EDITOR READ IT, AND...

I DON'T THINK I WANT IT IN THE PAPER.

WHAT?!!

Panel 8:
BUT IT'S ABOUT AN ESCAPE FROM EAST GERMANY! IT'S ABOUT COMING TO CANADA. IT'S ABOUT SURVIVAL! —IT'S A **GREAT** STORY!!

YES...AND WHOSE STORY IS IT, MR. PATTERSON? ...YOURS OR MINE?

Panel 9:
I CAN'T BELIEVE MR. BERGNER DOESN'T WANT THIS TO GO INTO THE STUDENT NEWSPAPER.

TOUGH, MAN. HE AGREED TO THE INTERVIEW, DIDN'T HE!

Panel 10:
I MEAN, WHEN YOU TALK TO A REPORTER, YOU'RE PUTTING INFORMATION INTO THE PUBLIC DOMAIN!

Panel 11:
BUT IT'S STILL HIS PERSONAL STORY. DOESN'T HE HAVE SOME SAY? DOESN'T HE HAVE THE RIGHT TO AT LEAST **READ** IT?

SURE!

Panel 12:
...BUT YOU PUBLISH IT FIRST.

JUNK! CLOTHES! FOOD! DISHES! - **IT NEVER ENDS!!**

YOU FINISH AT ONE END OF THE HOUSE AND YOU START AT THE OTHER! EVERY DAY, I CLEAN AND I TIDY AND I PICK UP AFTER **OTHER PEOPLE!**

MAN, IT'S AMAZING HOW FAST MOM CAN WORK WHEN SHE'S CHARGED!!

I AM EXHAUSTED TONIGHT. I REALLY DON'T FEEL LIKE COOKING.

SO, WHAT'S FOR DINNER?

TAKE-OUT.

...THERE'S FOOD IN THE FRIDGE. - OPEN IT UP, AND TAKE IT OUT.

WHAT A DAY I HAD TODAY! I LOST MY CAR KEYS, THEN THE CAR WOULDN'T START, SO BY THE TIME I GOT APRIL TO DAYCARE, I WAS LATE FOR WORK!

WE WERE SO BUSY AT THE STORE, I MISSED LUNCH, TRAFFIC WAS CRAZY, I DIDN'T HAVE TIME TO BUY GROCERIES BEFORE GETTING LIZ FROM CHOIR PRACTICE.... AND I CAME HOME TO CHAOS!!

I CAN'T WAIT TO CLIMB INTO BED AND TO FALL INTO A DEEP, PEACEFUL, WONDERFUL SLEEP!

YEAH...

AND, JUST THINK - IN 8 HOURS, THE CYCLE BEGINS ALL OVER AGAIN.

118

121

HEY, LIZARDBREATH!!

HEY, FUNGUS-FACE!

MICHAEL, YOU'VE LEFT YOUR WET JACKET ON THE HALL FLOOR—AND ARE ALL THESE GARBAGE BAGS **LAUNDRY**?!!

MAAAAH!!! EDGAR FREW UP INNA BAAAF-ROOOM EDGAR FREW UP INNA BAAF-ROOM!!

MAN, IT'S GOOD TO BE HOME!

IT'S GREAT TO SEE YOU HERE FOR MARCH BREAK, MIKE! I THOUGHT YOU WERE GONNA GO SKIING IN QUEBEC!

COULDN'T AFFORD IT, GORDO.

BESIDES, I HARDLY GET TO SEE RHETTA ANYMORE!

HOW'S IT GOING WITH YOU TWO?

GREAT! TRACEY AN' I HAVE BEEN TOGETHER FOR OVER TWO YEARS, NOW.

THAT'S A LONG TIME.

YEAH... I FIGURE, WHY TRADE 'ER IN WHEN SHE AIN'T RUSTED, AN' SHE STILL RUNS!

I HEAR YOU'VE TAKEN OVER DALY'S GARAGE, GORD!

YEAH! AN' TRACEY'S DOIN' ALL THE PAPER-WORK.

WE FIGURE IF WE REALLY PUT EVERYTHING INTO 'ER, SHE SHOULD BE A PRETTY GOOD BUSINESS!

TOGETHER?

...YOU'RE—GOING INTO THIS THING TOGETHER?

DON'T WORRY, MIKE... IT'S GONNA BE SORT OF AN UNLIMITED PARTNER-SHIP.

WHAT DO YOU MEAN BY UN-LIMITED?

WE'RE GETTING MARRIED!

Panel 1: MAN, I AM STUNNED!! GORDON AN' TRACEY... GETTING MARRIED?!
THEY NEVER SAID "WHEN", MIKE.

Panel 2: YEAH, BUT THEY'RE SO YOUNG! — I CAN'T EVEN IMAGINE GETTING MARRIED!
ME NEITHER. I WANT TO TRAVEL, TRY NEW THINGS, HAVE A PLACE OF MY OWN!

Panel 3: I DON'T PLAN TO GET MARRIED 'TIL 30, AT LEAST! I MEAN, YOU DON'T EVEN KNOW YOURSELF 'TIL THEN, SO HOW CAN YOU MAKE A LIFETIME COMMITMENT TO SOMEONE ELSE?!!
EXACTLY.

Panel 4: MICHAEL.... DO YOU THINK WE'LL EVER GET MARRIED?

Panel 5: WHAT?!!
THAT'S WHAT THEY SAID, MOM. TRACEY'S ALREADY STARTED TO FIX UP THE APARTMENT OVER DALY'S GARAGE.

Panel 6: WELL... I GUESS GORDON'S BEEN MAKING DECISIONS FOR HIMSELF ALL HIS LIFE ... AND TRACEY'S A MATURE AND SENSIBLE GIRL, BUT....
WEIRD ISN'T IT!

Panel 7: WHAT'S WEIRD?
TRACEY AN' GORDO ARE GONNA GET MARRIED.

Panel 8: I DUNNO WHY! ...IT SURE ISN'T SOMETHING THAT **I'M** GONNA DO FOR AWHILE!!!

Panel 9: WAS THAT A SIGH OF RELIEF?
NO.... IT WAS JUST A SIGH.

YES, SIR! — IF THERE'S ONE THING I'M LOOKING FORWARD TO ON THIS CRUISE WE'RE TAKING, IT'S THE **FOOD**!!

HEH, HEH, HEH.... YOU WANT A GOOD LAUGH, EL?

CHECK OUT THE "TYPICAL AMERICAN TOURISTS"!!

LOOK, JOHN... I BOUGHT THIS FOR ELIZABETH!

I THINK I'LL GET THAT PARROT FOR APRIL!

MICHAEL'S ALWAYS WANTED TO SEE REAL PALM TREES...

WOULDN'T THE KIDS LOVE THIS!

GRAMMA... ARE MOM AN' DAD COMING HOME SOON?

YES, DEAR.

...DO YOU THINK THEY MISSED US?

HI, CONNIE! —YES, WE HAD A GREAT TRIP— NOT A DULL MOMENT THE WHOLE TIME!!

WAIT 'TIL YOU SEE OUR PHOTOGRAPHS! —THE BEACHES WERE BEAUTIFUL, THE FOOD WAS TO DIE FOR... AND JOHN AND I DANCED FOR THE FIRST TIME IN AGES!!

UH HUH, WE WENT SNORKELING, WENT FOR A DONKEY RIDE, DID THE CASINOS—THE WHOLE BIT!

AND THEY SAID I COULDN'T COME WIF THEM, 'CAUSE THERE WAS NUFFING TO DO!!

WE HAD A COOL TIME WITH GRANDMA WHILE YOU GUYS WERE AWAY, MOM.

WE MADE CAKE AN' TAFFY AN' GINGERBREAD MEN.

SHE SAYS SHE NEVER HAS ANY TROUBLE WORKING IN SOMEONE ELSE'S KITCHEN... SHE JUST SORTA MAKES IT "HERS".

OH.

...THAT EXPLAINS WHY I CAN'T FIND ANYTHING!

MOM?) JUST A MINUTE, APRIL. I'M SHOWING CONNIE THE PICTURES FROM OUR CRUISE!

DADDY?) NOT NOW, HONEY—I'M ON THE PHONE.

AYPO, DO YOU WANT TO GO OUTSIDE? YES, I DO!) OK, YOU CAN GO!

WHAT ARE YOU DOING OUT HERE?

GRAMMA SAID IT WAS OK AS LONG AS I **ASKED** SOMEBODY.

AAAAHHH!
COUGH COUGH
MA-MAAA

GASP!!

BOWOW OW! BARK!
SCRATCH SCRATCH
BARK BARK BARK!

WELL, DON'T JUST STAND THERE, EDGAR... COME ON IN!

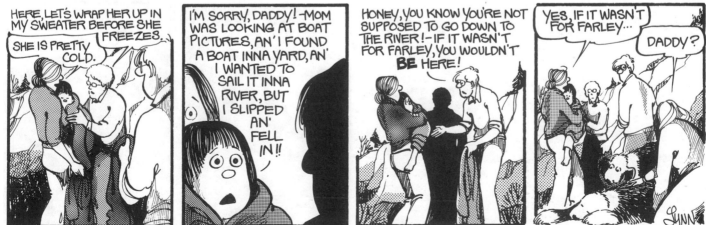

EPILOGUE

We received hundreds of letters when Farley died. Some telling me that it needn't have happened; some saying that it brought back fond memories of treasured pets whose love and companionship meant everything.

For me, it was a difficult story to write and illustrate, and it made me realize, once again, how strongly the people I work for identify and commiserate with these characters.

Though Farley lives on in the shape and spirit of "Edgar," I'll miss him too. He was just a figment of a cartoonist's imagination, but, in so many ways, he was real!

Lynn Johnston

Eau Claire District Library

OTHER FOR BETTER OR FOR WORSE® COLLECTIONS

"There Goes My Baby"
Things Are Looking Up
What, Me Pregnant?
If This Is a Lecture, How Long Will It Take?
Pushing 40
It's All Downhill From Here
Keep the Home Fries Burning
The Last Straw
Just One More Hug
"It Must Be Nice to Be Little"
Is This "One of Those Days," Daddy?
I've Got the One-More-Washload Blues

RETROSPECTIVES

It's the Thought That Counts: Fifteenth Anniversary Collection
For Better or For Worse: The 10th Anniversary Collection